FLAVORS OF THE WORLD

THE FOOD OF THAILAND

Patricia K. Kummer

Marshall Cavendish Benchmark
New York

Website: www.marshallcavendish.us

This publication represents the opinions and views of the author based on Patricia K. Kummer's personal experience, knowledge, and research. The information in this book serves as a general guide only. The author and publisher have used their best efforts in preparing this book and disclaim liability rising directly and indirectly from the use and application of this book.

Other Marshall Cavendish Offices:
Marshall Cavendish International (Asia) Private Limited, 1 New Industrial Road, Singapore 536196 • Marshall Cavendish International (Thailand) Co Ltd. 253 Asoke, 12th Flr, Sukhumvit 21 Road, Klongtoey Nua, Wattana, Bangkok 10110, Thailand • Marshall Cavendish (Malaysia) Sdn Bhd, Times Subang, Lot 46, Subang Hi-Tech Industrial Park, Batu Tiga, 40000 Shah Alam, Selangor Darul Ehsan, Malaysia

Marshall Cavendish is a trademark of Times Publishing Limited

All websites were available and accurate when this book was sent to press.

Library of Congress Cataloging-in-Publication Data

Kummer, Patricia K.
   The food of Thailand / Patricia K. Kummer.
        p. cm. — (Flavors of the world)
Summary: "Explores the culture, traditions, and festivals of Thailand through its food"—Provided by publisher.
Includes bibliographical references and index.
ISBN 978-1-60870-238-1 (print) ISBN 978-1-60870-691-4 (ebook)

   1.   Food habits—Thailand—Juvenile literature. 2. Festivals—Thailand—Juvenile literature. 3. Thailand—Social life and customs—Juvenile literature. I. Title.

GT2853.T5K86 2012
394.1'209593—dc22
2010023508

Editor: Christine Florie
Publisher: Michelle Bisson
Art Director: Anahid Hamparian
Series Designer: Kay Petronio

Expert Reader: Naam Pruitt, Thai chef, cookbook author, cooking instructor, Kirkwood, Missouri

Photo research by Marybeth Kavanagh

Cover photo by Lee Snider/The Image Works

The photographs in this book are used by permission and through the courtesy of: SuperStock: Eye Ubiquitous, 4; Robert Harding Picture Library, 15, 37, 54; Getty Images: DEA/C.DANI-I.JESKE, 8; Wai-Lam Chin/Image Bank, 9; Jerry Alexander/Lonely Planet Images, 22; Terry Williams, 46; MIB Pictures, 48; Ashok Sinha, 49; The Image Works: Lee Snider, 10; Jim Holmes/AA World Travel/Topfoto, 35; AP Photo: Apichart Weerawong, 17; Alamy: Peter Horree, 20; Barry Lewis, 27; Johnny Henshall, 30; Roger Cracknell 01/Classic, 33; Dave Shilton, 36; Dave Stamboulis, 42; Kevin Foy, 44; Robert Harding Picture Library Ltd, 47; Elena Nikolajeva, 50; Marc Anderson, 51; StockFood: Herbert Lehmann, 28; Fotolia: Rawich Liwlucksaneey (limes), front & back cover, 1; Alexstar (coconut), 3; Akhilesh Sharma (banner), front cover, 1, 3, 5, 19, 32, 41, 51; Sandra Cunningham (spices), 11, 23, 39, 43, 55; Shutterstock: Suto Norbert Zsolt (map), front cover, 1, 2-3, 13, 17, 21, 30, 37, 40, 47, 52; VectorStock: Nicemonkey (plate), back cover, 3

Maps (pp. 6 & 26) by Mapping Specialists Limited

Printed in Malaysia
1 3 5 6 4 2

CONTENTS

ONE

Rice Bowl of the World

||||||||||||||||||||||||||||||||||||||||||||||||||||||||||||||||||||||||||||||||||||

Forested mountains rise in the north. White-sand beaches line the coasts. Almost 2 million miles (3,218,600 kilometers) of waterways cut through valleys, plains, and plateaus on their way to the sea. Rich soil and a wet, warm tropical climate allow for year-round production of crops. Thailand is indeed an amazing country.

People first settled in this amazing land at least ten thousand years ago. They developed the first culture based on growing rice (*khao*). Between then and now, villages grew, kingdoms rose and fell, and the country that became Thailand was formed. The Thai people are proud that their country was never a colony of a western country. They refer to Thailand as the "Land of the Free."

The people of Thailand have been growing rice for thousands of years. Here, a man threshes harvested rice in a large bamboo basket.

TOPOGRAPHICAL MAP OF THAILAND

MYANMAR

TANEN RANGE

Doi Inthanon

Chiang Mai

LAOS

Ping R.

Wang R.

Yom R.

Nan R.

Mekong R.

THAILAND

Udon Thani (Udorn)

CHAO PHRAYA RIVER BASIN

PHETCHABUN RANGE

Khon Kaen

KHORAT PLATEAU

Chi R.

Mun R.

Ubon Ratchathani

Tha Chin R.

Chao Phraya R.

Nakhon Ratchasima (Khorat)

DANGREK RANGE

VIETNAM

CENTRAL PLAIN

Bangkok

Samut Prakan

CAMBODIA

Andaman Sea

Gulf of Thailand

South China Sea

Samui

Surat Thani

Nakhon Si Thammarat

Phuket

MALAY PENINSULA

Strait of Malacca

MALAYSIA

The Land and People

Thailand is the second-largest country in Southeast Asia. It covers 198,116 square miles (513,120 km). That makes it larger than the state of California. Thailand's Southeast Asian neighbors are Laos to the north and northeast, Cambodia to the southeast, Myanmar (formerly called Burma) to the north and west, and Malaysia to the south. The Andaman Sea forms the rest of Thailand's western border. The Gulf of Thailand borders the country on the east and south.

If you look closely at the map of Thailand, you will discover that it resembles an elephant's head. The northern region forms the forehead. The northeastern region forms the ears. From the central plains region, the elephant's mouth opens into the Gulf of Thailand. The southern region is its long trunk.

Each of these four regions has its own special land and water features, ethnic groups, and foods. The North is known for mild-tasting dishes, pork sausages, and sticky rice (*khao niew*). Thailand's hottest dishes are eaten in the Northeast. The people there also dry and pickle much of their food. The people of the Central Plain eat a wide variety of foods, including jasmine rice and **curry** dishes made with coconut milk. Thailand's spiciest foods are found in the South.

The North is known for its mountain ranges, now sparsely covered with evergreen and teak trees. Thailand's highest point is Doi Inthanon, at 8,514 feet (2,595 meters) above sea level. It rises near the North's major city, Chiang Mai. The Ping, Wang, Yom, and Nan rivers flow south out of the mountains. Khao niew and corn grow in small fields carved out of the mountainsides. Fruits such as lychees, longans, and mandarin oranges do well in the cool river valleys. Though apples, strawberries, peaches, and apricots are not native Thai fruits, they have become very popular and grow well in this region. Tea and coffee crops also flourish here. Much of the farming is done by people from several hill tribes. They originally came from other countries, such as Myanmar, Tibet, and China.

Lychees thrive in the river valleys of northern Thailand.

The Khorat Plateau is the main landform of the Northeast, also called Isan. The Mekong River separates Isan from Laos to the east. Huge catfish swim in this river. The Chi and Mun rivers often flood as they cut across the plateau's dry, sandy soil. Cassava, corn, and rice are the main crops grown in the Northeast. Cattle and pigs are important livestock in the region. People with Laotian and Khmer backgrounds make up the largest ethnic groups here.

The Central Plain has Thailand's richest soil. It was formed by rivers flowing from the North into the Chao Phraya River basin. A system of **klongs** brings water from the Chao Phraya River to the rice paddies. Farmers in this region harvest two crops of jasmine rice a year, making Thailand the world's largest exporter of that type of rice. Corn, sugarcane, and bananas are other major crops of the Central Plain. Chickens and ducks are the region's main livestock. People of Chinese origin make up the largest ethnic group in this region.

Rice paddies thrive in Thailand's Central Plain region.

Exotic fish are sold at the outdoor market on Phuket.

The mountainous Malay Peninsula forms the region of the South. White-sand beaches line the coasts and islands such as Phuket and Koh Samui. Huge limestone rock formations pop out of the sea on either side of the peninsula. Birds such as swiftlets make nests in the rocks. Shellfish, including many varieties of shrimp, mussels, oysters, scallops, and lobsters, and fish such as marlin, sea bass, and mackerel, swim in the peninsula's coastal waters. Sugarcane, pineapples, about twenty kinds of bananas, mangoes, mangosteens, rambutan, durian, papayas, oil palm and coconut trees, and coffee are the main food crops of the South.

Pad Kee Mao Muu (Drunken Noodles and Pork)

There are five recipes in this book. They are intended to be made and served together for a Thai dinner. Drunken Noodles, a popular, easy-to-make dish, would be one of several dishes in a Thai home-cooked meal. Because this dish contains noodles, Thai would use chopsticks to eat it. If you make Drunken Noodles as the only dish in a meal, it would serve only two. Be sure that an adult helps you with this recipe.

Ingredients

6 ounces rice stick noodles

2 tablespoons vegetable oil

1 clove garlic, crushed

2 small chili peppers, chopped

1 onion, thinly sliced

½ pound lean pork, ground

1 green pepper, finely chopped and seeded

1 tablespoon each dark soy sauce and light soy sauce

½ teaspoon sugar

1 tomato, cut into small wedges

2 tablespoons sweet basil leaves

Directions

Serves 4

1. Soak noodles in hot water for 15 minutes and then drain.
2. Heat oil in **wok**. Stir-fry garlic, chilies, and onion for 1 minute.
3. On high heat, add pork and stir-fry until browned.
4. Add and stir-fry green pepper, soy sauces, and sugar.
5. Add noodles and tomato wedges. Toss mixture for a few minutes, until noodles and tomatoes are heated through.
6. Sprinkle with basil leaves and serve in a large bowl.

Malays who follow Islam and people with Chinese backgrounds make up the main ethnic groups in the South region.

Tropical Climate

Lying south of the Tropic of Cancer, Thailand has a tropical climate with three seasons. The hot, wet season lasts from May through September. **Monsoon** winds from the southwest bring an average of 60 inches (152 centimeters) of rain to Thailand. From October through February, monsoon winds from the northeast blow dry, cool air over the country. During March through April, Thailand has a short hot and dry season with no winds.

Temperatures can reach highs of 100 degrees Fahrenheit (38 degrees Celsius) or more on the Khorat Plateau. The Malay Peninsula receives the most rainfall each year—up to 160 inches (406 cm). The high temperatures and plentiful rainfall allow Thai farmers to grow many tropical fruits. They also make Thailand the "Rice Bowl of the World" with high rice yields.

Early People

For at least ten thousand years, people have lived in what is now Thailand. In the Northeast, archaeologists have found rice that dates to 8000 BCE. They believe the people who grew it were the first in the world to cultivate rice. These early people also raised chickens and pigs and caught fish in the rivers.

Tsunami Disrupts Thailand's Food Production

On December 26, 2004, an earthquake occurred under the Indian Ocean. It caused a series of high, powerful waves, called a tsunami, to crash ashore on land along the Indian Ocean. At about 8 a.m. the waves hit the west coast of Thailand's Malay Peninsula. About eight thousand people in Thailand died during the tsunami.

Towns, resorts, and homes were destroyed. Food production was also affected. Farm fields and coconut and nut-tree plantations were torn up. Shrimp beds and fishing boats along the coast were destroyed. Thousands of Thai who worked on farms and as fishers were put out of work. Some of them had fished in the Andaman Sea for their living.

By 2010 most of the area had recovered from the damage, including the farming, shrimping, and fishing industries.

Over hundreds of years, people from neighboring lands moved into Thailand. By the 500s CE they had built farming villages. They traded with one another throughout the region. By the 900s CE Mon people from what is now Myanmar had established Theravada Buddhist kingdoms in central Thailand. Khmers from Cambodia had expanded their kingdom into eastern Thailand. On the Malay Peninsula a trading empire based in Indonesia created settlements.

By the 1000s CE ethnic Thai people from what is now northern Vietnam had moved into northern Thailand. They settled in river valleys, planted rice, fished from the rivers, and gathered other foods, such as lemongrass and galangal. They used water buffalo for plowing and raised chickens and pigs for food.

The Land of the Free

By the 1200s the Thai had pushed into the Chao Phraya River basin and onto the Malay Peninsula. They forced the Mons and Khmers out of what is now Thailand. Two Thai kingdoms were formed in the North—Lanna, with Chiang Mai as its capital, and Sukhothai. An early Sukhothai king had an inscription carved in stone in the Thai language. Part of it said, "This land of Sukhothai is thriving. There is fish in the water and rice in the fields."

In 1351 the Thai kingdom of Ayutthaya was founded. Its capital was north of present-day Bangkok. By 1450 the rulers gained control of most of what is now Thailand. Theravada Buddhism became the official religion. An elaborate cooking style developed that became known as royal Thai **cuisine**. Recipes were written down and followed for centuries. Trade opened with China, India, and European countries. Curries came from India; noodles, from China. The Portuguese brought chili peppers from South America.

Barges fill the harbor in sixteenth-century Ayutthaya, a place where trade with other countries flourished.

They also taught the palace chefs how to make pastries with eggs, flour, and sugar and how to make omelets. Other European traders brought corn, eggplant, potatoes, and tomatoes from the Americas. Carrots, peas, and asparagus were also introduced.

In 1767 Burma destroyed the Ayutthayan kingdom. Four years later the Thai pushed out the Burmese. By 1782 the Thai had expanded their territory into Burma, Cambodia, Laos, and the Malay Peninsula. In that year a new king, Rama I, moved the capital to Bangkok and founded the Chakri dynasty. This dynasty continues today with the rule of Rama IX, also know as King Bhumibol Adulyadej.

Many changes occurred in Thailand between 1782 and today. In the early 1800s rice, sugarcane, and cassava became major export corps. A network of klongs was built to get these crops to the port of Bangkok. Rama IV adopted western customs such as using forks and spoons. In the late 1800s and early 1900s, Rama V gave up Thailand's land in Laos and Cambodia to France and land in Burma and part of the Malay Peninsula to Britain. However, he maintained what is Thailand today.

By the 1930s many Thai wanted a voice in their government. In 1932 they staged a peaceful revolt that ended with the creation of a constitutional **monarchy**. The king remained in place, but the government was run by a prime minister and an elected parliament. In 1939 the head of the government officially made *Thailand* the name of the country. Until then it had been called Siam by the rest of the world. After World War II (1939–1945) Thailand became an ally of the United States.

As Thailand has developed ties with the West, western eating styles have come into the country. In the 1970s, U.S. troops stationed in Thailand during the Vietnam War

King Bhumibol

King Bhumibol (1927–present) was born in Cambridge, Massachusetts, and went to school in Switzerland. Upon the death of his older brother, who had been the king of Thailand, Bhumibol became king. King Bhumibol is the world's longest-reigning monarch (1946–present). He is not only highly respected but deeply loved by his people.

King Bhumibol has done much to improve the life and health of the Thai people. He set up experimental rice fields, a rice mill, fish ponds, and a dairy farm on the palace grounds in Bangkok. What is learned there is shared with Thailand's farmers. In 1962 he made the recipes known as royal Thai cuisine available to all the Thai people.

introduced hamburgers, French fries, Coca-Cola, and 7-Up. More recently, McDonald's, KFC, and barbecued rib restaurants have been introduced. Italian pizzerias and pasta restaurants have also become popular.

In turn, Thailand influences eating all around the world. It is the world's largest exporter of jasmine rice and is a major exporter of frozen shrimp, canned tuna and pineapple, and ready-to-eat rice, fish, and curry dishes. In recent years Thai cuisine has become one of the world's most popular. Thousands of Thai restaurants have opened in countries in Asia, Europe, and the Americas. Many people in these regions now make Thai dishes at home.

TWO

Four Regions, Many Foods

||||||||||||||||||||||||||||||||||||||||||||||||||||||||||||||||||||||||||||||||||||||||||||||||||

Thai food appeals to all five senses. First, it balances flavors that tickle the taste buds—sweet, sour, hot, bitter, and salty. Coconut milk, fruits, and cane and palm sugar provide a sweet taste. **Fermented** vegetables, lime juice, tamarind, and vinegar give a sour taste. Chilies and peppercorns give Thai food its hot, spicy kick. Bitter melons and kaffir limes leave a bitter taste. Fish sauce (*nam pla*) made from anchovies and shrimp paste, used in curry pastes, provides the salty taste, much as soy sauce does for Chinese foods. Second, herbs and spices such as basil, coriander, cumin, galangal, garlic, ginger, lemongrass, lime leaves, mint, and turmeric awaken the sense of smell. Third, the colorful curry sauces, salads, and fruits appeal to the sense of sight. Fourth, the sense of feel or touch comes into play as smooth sauces and crisp vegetables are eaten and as sticky rice is rolled into balls. Finally, the sense of hearing is used as conversation and laughter take place around the Thai table.

Thai people think that life, including food and eating, should be *sanuk*—fun!

Basic Thai Foods: Rice, Curries, and Dipping Sauces

The staple of the Thai diet is rice. Thai greet each other by saying, "Have you eaten rice yet today?" This greeting is most often heard in rural areas. Thai begin their meals with a spoonful of rice. To their rice they then add a few spoonfuls at a time of other foods—stir-fried vegetables and small portions of chicken, pork, beef, and fish or shellfish curries.

Thailand's Buddhist monks eat their midday meal of rice, along with a variety of other dishes.

How to Cook Thai Rice

Thai cooks make two kinds of rice—long-grain jasmine rice and short-grain sticky, or glutinous, rice. For jasmine rice, a cook brings equal parts of rice and water to a boil in a covered pot. Then, the cook uncovers the pot and stirs until the water is below the rice. Next, the cook covers the pot, turns the heat to low, and lets the rice steam for about twenty minutes. The result is light, fluffy rice. Electric rice cookers now make preparing jasmine rice much easier. This rice is eaten by people in the Central Plain and in the South.

Short-grain sticky rice is first soaked in water for several hours. The cook puts the rice in a bamboo steamer basket that is placed over a metal pot of boiling water. With the heat turned to medium, the cook puts a lid over the rice and lets it steam for about thirty minutes. The gluten in the short-grain rice causes the cooked rice to be sticky. This is the only rice eaten by people in the North and Northeast. Throughout Thailand, this rice is used in khanom—the Thai term for a sweet dessert.

The Thai grow both long-grain jasmine rice and short-grain sticky rice. Excess short-grain rice is milled into flour, which in turn is used to make rice noodles. Noodles are used in soups, salads, and stir-fried dishes.

Curry brings Thai food to life. In Thailand, curry is a soupy stew. It can be made in many different ways, depending on the

Curry is an important element of Thai cooking. Above are four Thai curries and their ingredients.

ingredients used. The type of curry paste and the meat, fish, or vegetables can vary. So can the cooking liquid—coconut milk or water. The Thai make six basic kinds of curry paste: green (hottest), red (mild to hot), yellow (mild, sweet, and spicy), orange (sour), panang (hot), and massaman (sweet). The common ingredient is chilies. About twelve varieties of chilies grow in Thailand. Fresh green chilies are used in green curry paste, while dried red chilies are used in the other pastes. To make the curry paste, chilies, galangal, lemongrass, kaffir lime leaves, garlic, shallots, and shrimp paste are ground together using a **mortar and pestle**.

Kaeng Kari Kai
(Yellow Chicken Curry)

For this dish you must make a curry paste. Place the paste you don't use in a tightly closed container, and store it in the refrigerator until you make another curry. To complete this dish, you must also make jasmine rice using the instructions on page 21, How to Cook Thai Rice. If you make yellow chicken curry as the only dish for a meal, it will serve only two. Again, be sure an adult helps you with this recipe.

Ingredients

2 tablespoons vegetable oil

1 tablespoon curry paste (Mix 4 ounces yellow curry, 1 tablespoon curry powder, 1-1/2 teaspoons turmeric powder, and 1 teaspoon vegetable oil into a paste.)

1 cup raw chicken breast, cubed

2 tablespoons shallots, chopped

½ cup each potatoes and plum tomatoes, cubed

1 cup each unsweetened coconut milk and water

1-1/2 tablespoons fish sauce

1-1/2 teaspoons sugar

Directions

Serves 4

1. Heat oil in a wok over medium-high heat. Add curry paste and stir-fry about 30 seconds.
2. Add chicken and stir-fry about 1 minute, until nearly cooked.
3. Add shallots and potatoes and stir-fry about 3 minutes.
4. Add tomato pieces, coconut milk, water, fish sauce, and sugar. Cook until sauce thickens, about 15 minutes. If too thick, add more coconut milk. Taste to see if more fish sauce or sugar should be added.
5. Spoon into a serving dish, and serve with jasmine rice.

Additional herbs and spices are ground up to give each curry paste its own flavor and heat. In a wok the curry paste is stirred into a small amount of hot cooking oil. Then meat, chicken, or fish and some vegetables are added and stir-fried. Coconut milk or water is added and heated to complete the curry dish. Thai then spoon the curry over their rice.

Dipping sauces served in saucers provide seasonings for Thai food. Fish sauce with slices of fresh red and green chilies is used in the same way Americans use salt and pepper. Shrimp and other seafood are dipped in a sauce of lime juice, sugar, and minced garlic. Meat, chicken, and vegetables each have their own traditional dipping sauces.

Although the same basic ingredients are used throughout the country, each region has its own ways of using and serving them. Also, each region has its own specialty dishes.

Foods of the North

The Thai in the North prefer the least spicy of foods. Sticky rice is the only rice eaten there. The northern Thai pick up sticky rice and roll it into a small ball between the thumb and the first two fingers of their right hand. Then they use the ball of rice to scoop up meats and vegetables in curry dishes. Curry in the North is mild and is mainly made with vegetable or meat broths instead of coconut milk. Egg noodles are more popular than rice noodles in the North because many people with

Chinese backgrounds live there. Noodles are served with beef and chicken curries.

The North is known for its pork sausages. A red curry paste blended with ground pork makes a spicy red sausage. A sour-tasting sausage is made from ground pork, pork rind, salt, garlic, and chilies. It is pressed into a clay pot, where the salt and chilies "cook" the pork. This sausage must be eaten within a few days. In northern cities and villages, vendors sell roasted corn on the cob.

People in the rural North have their own style of eating, called *khan tohk*. At home, they sit on the floor around a round table (tohk) with a raised edge. Various meat and vegetable dishes are served in small, lidded bowls (khans). Sticky rice is served in individual woven baskets. At the end of the meal, fruits such as lychee and longan might be served.

Northeast (Isan) Foods

Isan is the poorest region in Thailand. The dry, sandy soil and limited rainfall make it difficult for farmers to grow crops. On the northern part of the Khorat Plateau, sticky rice is the main crop. South of the Mun River, jasmine rice is the main crop. Throughout Isan people in rural areas eat sticky rice, while people in cities prefer jasmine rice.

Because meat is scarce in the Northeast, it is eaten in small amounts within hot, spicy curries. Freshwater fish from rivers and land crabs found in rice fields are the main sources of protein.

THE FOOD REGIONS OF THAILAND

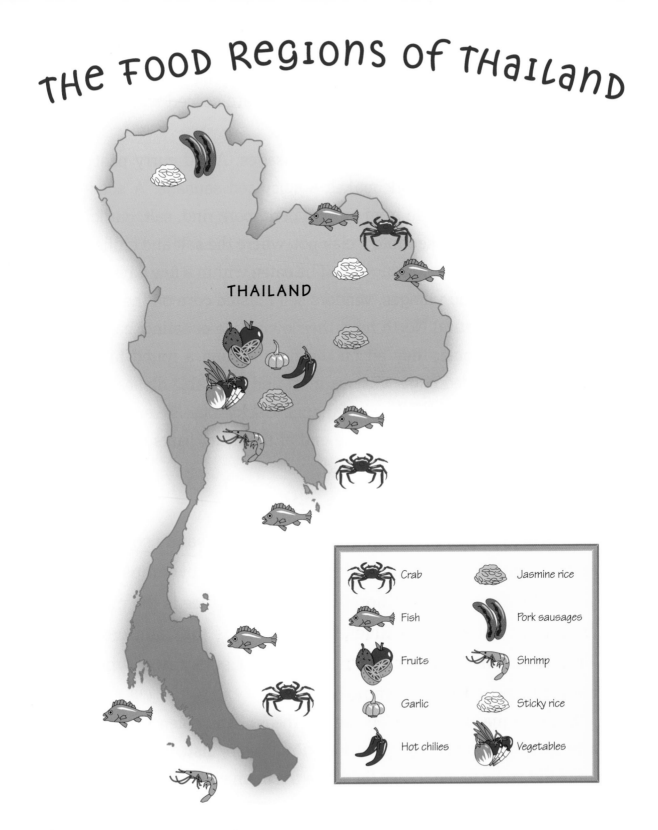

THAILAND

Legend:

- Crab
- Fish
- Fruits
- Garlic
- Hot chilies
- Jasmine rice
- Pork sausages
- Shrimp
- Sticky rice
- Vegetables

Men from the Akha tribe eat food from khans around a tohk.

Because fresh foods are not available year round, people on the plateau preserve food by drying or pickling it. Fish and crabs are sometimes pounded into pastes and dried. A dish called *laap* helps to stretch the protein. Minced meat, chicken, duck, or fish is tossed with lime juice, fish sauce, chilies, mint leaves, and shallots as the laap is cooked.

Some foods from Isan that might seem strange to westerners include deep-fried bamboo worms that are nutty and crunchy and grasshoppers that taste like fish. A green plant that grows

Thai of Isan enjoy snacking on deep-fried bamboo worms dipped in chili sauce.

on top of ponds is high in protein, vitamins, and minerals. The people of Isan add it to salads or stir-fry it with oil and garlic.

Foods of the Central Plain

The basics of Thai cuisine were developed in this region—rice, fish, vegetables, fish sauce, and curries flavored with black pepper, hot chilies, and garlic. This happened because the Central Plain has the best soil and climate in Thailand. It is the main area for growing jasmine rice, which is the main food of the Central Plain. Vegetables such as Thai eggplant, bamboo shoots, snake beans, tomatoes, water spinach, and lotus shoots flourish in the region. Fruits such as custard apples, durians, guavas, mangoes, and pomelos are in great supply. Freshwater fish, shrimp, and crabs are found in the rivers, canals, and rice paddies.

Because of the abundant food supply, meals are often elaborate and include several kinds of foods. Dishes made with red, green, and panang curries—all made with coconut milk—are preferred in this region. Lemongrass and chili soup and chicken coconut soup are favorites. Hot and tangy salads made with lime juice, chilies, lettuce, lemongrass, mint leaves, and roasted vegetables, noodles, meat, or seafood are popular. Dishes flavored with palm sugar are also preferred in the Central Plain region.

Chinese–Thai foods are found in Central Plain's cities, especially in Bangkok. These foods include noodle dishes and braised meats.

Bangkok

Bangkok is the capital of Thailand and is located in the Central Plain region. About 10 percent of Thailand's 66 million people live in this city. Cooking styles from all of Thailand's regions can be found in Bangkok.

Bangkok is also the home of royal Thai cuisine, which incorporates many Chinese and Indian cooking techniques. Many restaurants specialize in these elaborate foods, such as roast duck with red curry. Other restaurants specialize in French, Italian, American, Mexican, Korean, Chinese, Japanese, or Indian foods.

Besides hundreds of restaurants, Bangkok is known for its round-the-clock food stalls. People can buy something to eat at any time of the day or night. Pad Thai is a favorite one-dish meal that's good anytime.

Pad Thai

Pad Thai was created so that Bangkok's office workers could grab a tasty, nutritious snack. In Thailand it is served as a snack by street vendors. Pad Thai is usually not made in Thai homes, but it is a quick and easy stir-fry dish. The following ingredients are stir-fried in a small amount of vegetable oil: softened rice noodles, shrimp, egg, cubed tofu, Chinese chives, bean sprouts, roasted peanuts, shallots, and garlic. A warm sauce of tamarind juice, fish sauce, and sugar is added to the mixture.

Foods of the South

Because Thai on the peninsula are surrounded by water, they enjoy a greater variety of fish and seafood than do people to the north. Fish is grilled outdoors over charcoal or is used in stir-fried and curry dishes.

Thai on the Malay Peninsula are quite different from those in the main part of Thailand. Their foods reflect these differences, with their bright colors and spiciness. All curries in the South tend to be spicier than those in Thailand's other regions. About 80 percent of southern Thai have Malay backgrounds and follow Islam rather than Buddhism. Muslims prefer sweet, spicy massaman curries that include cardamom, cumin, and cloves. An especially popular Muslim dish is *satay*—pieces of chicken grilled on a stick, served with a rich peanut sauce. Muslims also make many dishes with lamb. Their religion forbids them to eat pork.

A great number of Chinese people live in the South's cities. They prefer rice noodles, pork, barbecued meats, steamed buns, and dumplings. The Buddhist minority in the South enjoys yellow curries made with turmeric and coconut milk.

THREE

Daily Life

||||||||||||||||||||||||||||||||||||||||||||||||||||||||||||||||||||||||||||||||||||||||||||

Thai in both rural and urban areas lead busy lives that often revolve around home, school, and work. During the past thirty years, cities with apartments, condominiums, office buildings, and factories have increased in size and population. Thousands of people from the Northeast have moved to Bangkok in search of better educations and jobs. Others have moved to cities in the South, where many have found work in the fishing industry. Many city workers have low-paying factory jobs and live in run-down neighborhoods. People with higher incomes live in single-family homes in suburbs.

About 66 percent of Thailand's people still live in rural villages. About 42 percent of them are farmers or fishers; others work in local markets (**talaats**). Still others work in small rice mills, fish-processing plants, or other factories. Most farmers own their land. Some farmers in the Northeast are tenant farmers who rent from a landlord. Although most farmers do not make a great deal of money, they are considered well off because they grow their own food. Many farmers in the South work for wages on sugarcane and pineapple plantations.

Lifestyles in Thailand

In rural parts of Thailand that are prone to flooding, wooden houses are built on stilts. The kitchen is under the house, and the living, eating, and sleeping area is reached by stairs. Houses built more recently are made of concrete or cinder block and sit on the ground. In the cities most people live in apartment buildings. Sometimes a family lives in a one-bedroom unit, cooks on the balcony, and shares a bathroom with other families.

A woman prepares a meal in a wok at the Bangkok Floating Market.

In recent years electricity has reached many rural areas, and with it electric rice cookers, radios, and television sets. However, cooking in a wok over a charcoal burner remains the main way of cooking in rural areas and in some parts of cities. Running water has become more common in rural areas. In many places, however, rainwater is still collected in barrels or pumped from a well, and the toilet is outside or is a hole in the ground.

Along the coasts, rivers, and canals, Thai get around in long-tail boats and motorboats. On land many Thai still walk, while others take buses, ride bicycles or motorcycles, or drive cars. There are eight times more motorcycles than cars in Thailand.

Family ties in Thailand are strong. Grandparents, parents, and children sometimes live in the same house. Children are brought up to respect their elders. Adults remain at home until they marry and usually have finished their education before then. In rural areas everyone shares in the farm and household chores. Children learn at an early age how to cut food in preparation for cooking.

Markets and Gardens

Villages and neighborhoods in the cities have talaats. Fresh fruits, vegetables, meats, poultry, and fish are set out for sale early in the morning. The grandmother, mother, or daughters in a family shop for foods needed for the day's meals. By early afternoon, most of the food has been sold. Even though many homes now have refrigerators, Thai like to eat fresh foods.

Thailand's cities also have modern supermarkets. Now that many women work outside the home, they often stop at a supermarket to pick up processed and ready-to-eat foods. This saves time at home because they don't have to cut up all the ingredients into bite-size pieces.

The Thai talaat is an open-air market where fresh products can be purchased.

Besides markets, most Thai—especially in villages—grow food in their own gardens. They grow basil, chili peppers, coriander, galangal, kaffir limes, and lemongrass. Some Thai also grow banana, custard apple, jackfruit, mango, and papaya trees in their yards.

Modern supermarkets can be found in the urban areas of Thailand.

The Floating Market

At one time Bangkok was known as the Venice of Asia because of its many canals. Now most of them have been paved over to make room for streets and buildings. West of the city the remaining canals support the Floating Market. Women travel the waters in long-tail boats loaded with fresh fruits, vegetables, and flowers for sale.

Meals

Thai eat small amounts of food all day, with dinner being the main meal. The main dish in a Thai dinner is rice. Everything else—soup, salad, curry, and dipping sauces—is considered a side dish that complements the rice. All dishes are served at the same time—not in courses—on a mat on the floor. Some Thai in cities now use western-style tables and chairs. Each person receives his or her own plate of rice and bowl of soup, a spoon, and a fork. Thai use the fork to push food onto the spoon, from which they eat. Because the ingredients are in bite-size pieces, knives are unnecessary. Chopsticks are used only for noodle dishes and in Chinese homes. Traditionally, Thai do not end meals with dessert. Instead, fresh fruit is served. Even in most Thai restaurants, desserts are not on the menu. Under western influence, however, some restaurants now offer cakes, pastries, and ice cream. The beverage of choice in Thai homes is bottled water.

Breakfast might include boiled eggs, fried rice, or leftovers from dinner the night before, such as a bowl of fish or beef soup. Workers on their way to the office or factory might stop at a street vendor for a bowl of *johk*. This is rice porridge with pork, coriander, shallots, and shredded ginger. Sometimes an egg is added.

Today, most children eat a hot lunch at school. Servers ladle up bowls of rice and soup to which the students add sauces for flavoring. Noodle dishes and soups from street vendors are popular lunch dishes with workers in cities. Other workers eat lunch at restaurants.

During morning and afternoon breaks, workers and students purchase snacks. They might have a bowl of soup or

Thom Preowan Thao Hu (Sweet and Sour Tofu Soup)

This recipe makes the soup dish for your Thai meal. It has a blend of sweet and sour tastes and a variety of textures. Thai do not eat soup directly from the bowl. Instead, they spoon small amounts onto their rice, thus adding flavor to the rice. As always, be sure an adult helps you with this recipe.

Ingredients

5 cups vegetable stock

1 tablespoon cornstarch

2-1/2 ounces pickled cabbage, chopped

2-1/2 ounces bamboo shoots, thinly sliced

5 ears baby corn, cut crosswise

4 ounces silken tofu, cubed

½ cup crabmeat

2 tablespoons light soy sauce

2 tablespoons fish sauce

1 tablespoon white vinegar

1 teaspoon sugar

Cilantro leaves

Directions

Serves 4

1. In a large saucepan, bring stock to a boil.
2. In a small bowl, mix a tablespoon of stock with the cornstarch. Stir this mixture into the rest of the stock and let it thicken.
3. Add the rest of the ingredients, except the cilantro. Stir well.
4. Ladle soup into four bowls and top with cilantro.

The Cost of Eating Out

Thai buy many foods, snacks, small meals, and drinks at markets, from street vendors, and in small restaurants. The chart below shows the cost in Thai bahts and U.S. dollars of some common purchases. As of November 2010, $1.00 equals about 32.4 bahts.

Food	Bahts	Cost in U.S. Dollars
One dish, such as fried noodles, a salad, curry, or seafood in a small restaurant	30–200B	$0.92–6.17
Sweets, desserts	15–50B	$0.47–1.55
Cup of soup	8B	$0.25
Meal of curry dishes, rice, fruit drink, and dessert at a night market	150B	$4.62
Plastic bottle of water	10B	$0.31
Bottle of soda pop	25B	$0.77

a dessert, such as sticky rice and mangoes. Workers also purchase sweet drinks, tea, and coffee. All-night markets provide foods for people on their way home from a movie, concert, or other evening activity.

FOUR

Celebrations, Festivals, and Holidays

||||||||||||||||||||||||||||||||||||||||||||||||||||||||||||||||||||||||||||||||||||||||

It is hard to find a week in Thailand when some regional, national, or religious festival or holiday is not being celebrated. In addition, families have their own special events—birth celebrations, weddings, and funerals. Rice plays an important role in most of these celebrations.

Religious Traditions

More than 90 percent of Thai follow Theravada Buddhism. This form of Buddhism emphasizes the important position of monks. Every young Buddhist male is expected to spend a three-month period as a monk in a nearby **wat** (temple). When a man begins his time as a monk, his family prepares a feast, which includes rice, curry dishes, hot and spicy salads, and a variety of sweets. They share the food with the monks at the monastery.

Monks eat twice a day, in the early morning and before noon. Every morning monks stop at homes and shops along village

Newly ordained monks feast on a variety of Thai specialties.

and city streets accepting food as **alms**. People place small packages of food (rice, curry) in the monks' bowls. When the bowls are full, the monks return to the monastery, divide their food, eat breakfast, and save food for the second meal. Thai who give food to the monks gain **merit**—rewards toward a better position in the next life.

Man Gaeng Buad
(Sweet Potatoes in Coconut Milk)

Although a traditional Thai meal might end with a plate of cut-up fresh fruit, man gaeng buad is a richer yet simple-to-make Thai dessert. Be sure an adult helps you with this recipe.

Ingredients

1 pound sweet potatoes, cut into 1-inch cubes

1 teaspoon salt

2-3/4 cups coconut cream

1/3 cup palm sugar (similar to brown sugar)

1-1/4 cups water

Directions

Serves 4

1. Place sweet potatoes in cold water. Add salt. Soak for 30 minutes and then drain.
2. In a saucepan, heat coconut cream. Add sweet potatoes and bring to a boil.
3. Add palm sugar and stir until it dissolves.
4. Add 1-1/4 cups water. Return mixture to boil, then simmer until sweet potatoes are tender. Don't let them get soft and mushy.
5. Ladle the dessert into bowls, and serve warm.

Buddhist monks receive early morning alms in Bangkok.

Buddhist monks provide many services to their followers. They bless new homes and businesses and present blessings at weddings and funerals. After each of these ceremonies, the monks are given food to eat.

Many Buddhists also practice **animism**, which is a belief in spirits. Each home, place of work, school, and center of a town or village has a spirit house. This looks like a small temple in which the earth's spirits can reside. To keep the spirits happy, people leave daily gifts of flowers, incense, and food such as rice, fruits, sweets, and cups of water or tea.

Thailand's Muslims observe Ramadan, a month of fasting. They eat and drink nothing from sunrise to sunset, and then they eat a light meal. At the end of Ramadan, they feast for three days during Eid al-Fitr.

Special Family Events

When a baby is born, the Buddhist family places a food offering on a banana leaf. This is supposed to protect the child from spirits. At the age of three months, babies are taken to the wat for a cleansing ceremony. Gifts of special foods are presented to the monks.

Buddhist wedding ceremonies and parties can last for twenty-four hours. First, as many as nine monks bless the couple. Then the monks and guests eat a meal at the bride's home. Later, the two families go to the groom's home, where they might have a thick soup of polished rice. In the North a rich Burmese curry is served at rural weddings. In the cities wedding receptions are sometimes held at hotels, where *luuk chup* is a special treat. This sweet made of soybean paste, sugar, and coconut milk is colored and shaped to look like small apples, carrots, cherries, chilies, eggplants, and grapes.

Buddhist funerals last from five to seven days and take place in the home of the deceased or in the wat. Monks chant and give blessings. The family provides food for the mourners and the monks to eat. When the funeral ends, the coffin and body are taken to be cremated (burned). Along the way, mourners throw

A variety of luuk chup is displayed at a market in Bangkok. Sometimes these colorful treats are offered at weddings.

grains of rice, which are believed to ease the deceased's path to the next life.

National Holidays and Festivals

Many national holidays revolve around the royal family. The anniversary of King Bhumibol Adulyadej's coronation is May 5. Also in early May the Royal Plowing Ceremony marks the start of the rice-planting season. On August 12 Thai celebrate Queen Sirikit's birthday, which has become Mother's Day in Thailand. Later in the year Father's Day is celebrated on December 5, which is the king's birthday. On these two occasions Thai might enjoy steamed chicken with a hot pepper dipping sauce and perhaps sliced roasted pork with dipping sauce in addition to rice and other dishes.

The Thai people have three new year's celebrations. On January 1 they eat son-in-law eggs—deep-fried, shelled boiled eggs that

Fruit and Vegetable Carving

Fruit and vegetable carving is one of the ten traditional Thai crafts. It began at the Sukhothai court. Today, even at an ordinary family dinner, carrots carved as leaves or tomatoes carved as roses may grace a plate of food. Girls are taught carving at school. Cucumbers, melons, onions, pineapples, mangoes, and eggplants

are some of the fruits and vegetables used for carving.

A New Year's treat eaten in Thailand is son-in-law eggs.

are cut in half; drizzled with a mixture of fish sauce, tamarind juice, and palm sugar; and sprinkled with slices of fried red chilies and onions. Chinese New Year arrives later in January or February. From April 13 through 15 Thai celebrate the Songkran festival. It marks the old Thai new year. Thai return to their hometowns for family reunions. Water plays an important role in Songkran, which comes at the height of the hot, dry season. Water is used to clean homes and public places and to wash away the sins of the past year. Scented water is sprinkled on statues of Buddha and on older family members by people looking to receive blessings. For fun, young people throw water or shoot it with water cannons at one another. A favorite food for Songkran is galloping horses—stir-fried ground pork topped with a red chili slice and cilantro leaf, all atop a piece of pineapple.

Loi Krathong, the Floating Lantern Festival, takes place during the full moon in November. Thai young and old place candles in small bamboo boats decorated with flowers and let them float down Thailand's rivers. The boats are supposed to carry away bad deeds. At the end of the ceremony Thai enjoy grilled chicken and fish as well as coconuts.

Loi Krathong, the Floating Lantern Festival, is celebrated each November in Thailand.

Regional Festivals

Individual towns and provinces also hold festivals throughout the year. In early May the town of Yasothon in the Northeast holds the Rocket Festival. Tall rockets are shot into the sky

What Is a Rambutan?

Rambutan is a fruit that grows in the area around Surat Thani on the Malay Peninsula. Under its red, hairy exterior lays sweet, juicy white flesh.

to awaken the gods that bring rain and thus a good rice crop. Chonburi in the Central Plain holds buffalo races in October.

Some towns hold festivals honoring a locally grown fruit—bananas in Kamphaeng Phet, custard apples in Nakhon Ratchasima, grapes in Ratchaburi, longans in Lamphun, lychees in Chiang Rai, mangoes in Chachoengsao, and rambutans in Surat Thani. For many of these festivals, locals select a queen and hold parades.

The Chinese communities in Bangkok and especially in Phuket in the South hold the Vegetarian Festival for nine days in late September or early October. It marks the observance of a Taoist custom in which the Chinese do not eat any kind of meat. During this time they eat only fruits, vegetables, mushrooms, tofu, noodles, and rice.

FIVE

Health and Nutrition

Thai cuisine is one of the world's healthiest. The Thai diet includes the same ratio of foods as is recommended in the USDA Food Pyramid. Rice and noodles form the basis of the Thai diet.

Great amounts of fresh fruits and vegetables are served with most meals. Small amounts of red meat, which are high in "bad" **cholesterol**, are eaten. Greater amounts of fish and shellfish, which are high in "good" cholesterol, make up the Thai diet. At home, small amounts of plant-based oils are used in cooking. Thai do not eat dairy products, such as milk, butter, and cheese. These foods are all high in fat and "bad" cholesterol.

The Thai diet includes very healthy ingredients such as fresh fruits and vegetables and small portions of red meat.

What Is Cholesterol?

The body produces cholesterol, a waxy, fatlike substance. Foods with animal fats—meat, poultry, fish, shellfish, lard, and dairy products—also have cholesterol. There are two types of cholesterol. Bad cholesterol clogs the arteries. This causes the heart to work harder to pump blood to all parts of the body. A heart attack or a stroke can result. Good cholesterol, on the other hand, helps keep the arteries clear and protects against heart disease.

Of course, Thai cuisine also has a dark side. The large quantity of salt, added mainly through fish sauce and shrimp paste, can cause high blood pressure. Eating too many dishes that are high in fat from coconut milk and coconut cream can lead to weight problems. Consuming too many deep-fried foods can also pack on the pounds.

Malnutrition

Although most Thai eat a wide variety of healthy foods, some people in the country suffer from malnutrition. They do not eat enough foods rich in vitamins, minerals, and protein. Many people in the North and Northeast regions eat too little protein. The sticky rice they eat there is low in that nutrient. The jasmine rice eaten in the rest of the country has a higher protein content. Because many people in the two northern regions are poor, they cannot afford meats and eggs, which are also sources of protein. Women and children in those regions are often deficient in iron. Meat is a good source of this mineral, as are green, leafy vegetables, which are not readily available in those regions. Vitamin A, which is found in carrots, sweet potatoes, cantaloupe, and dark green, leafy vegetables, is also lacking in their diets.

In recent years the Thai government has sponsored programs to reduce malnutrition. One program encourages women and children to drink soy milk made from protein-rich soybeans. Iron and other nutrients are added to this milk. Other programs help farmers and other rural people to grow healthy foods in their gardens.

Obesity

At the other end of the spectrum is the problem of **obesity**. This is caused by overeating or by eating the wrong foods. Obesity is mainly a problem in Thailand's cities, but it is on the rise in rural areas, too. Thai are buying more deep-fried foods and sweets from street vendors. In Thai cities more than two hundred western-owned supermarkets sell prepared foods for use at home. Home cooks thus use fewer fresh ingredients in meals.

Many Thai are also getting less exercise. Office workers and factory workers drive, take a bus, or ride a motorcycle to work. On the way home they pick up snacks. When they get home,

Though many Thai foods are healthy, the overeating of deep-fried foods can lead to obesity.

they become couch potatoes. All of these changes in lifestyle are causing unhealthy weight gains. A rise in type 2, or adult-onset, diabetes has resulted from the increased fat and sugar intake and the decrease in exercise.

Obesity is also on the rise among Thai children and teenagers in the cities. They pick up snacks at school and on the way home and then watch television or play video games. As schools in the United States are doing, Thai schools are trying to make healthier snacks available. They are also encouraging young people to walk or bicycle and to take part in sports.

Som Tam

(Green Papaya Salad)

Som tam is a favorite diet food in Thailand. It has very little fat but is tasty and filling. The papaya provides vitamin C, folic acid, and potassium. You can make this salad as a one-dish meal for one person or as the salad for your four-person Thai dinner. Be sure an adult helps you with this recipe.

Ingredients

3 bird's-eye chilies

3 cloves garlic

½ cup string beans, cut in 1-inch pieces

2 tablespoons roasted peanuts

1 tablespoon dried shrimp

3 cherry tomatoes, cut in half

1 tablespoon fish sauce

1-1/2 tablespoons lime juice

1 tablespoon palm sugar

1-1/2 cups green papaya, shredded

Large cabbage leaves

(Note: For a milder som tam, use fewer chilies.)

Directions

Serves 4

1. Use a mortar and pestle to mash chilies and garlic together. Move to a mixing bowl.
2. Add string beans, peanuts, dried shrimp, and tomatoes.
3. Season with fish sauce, lime juice, and palm sugar.
4. Add shredded papaya, and gently toss all ingredients together.
5. Serve on a plate on a large cabbage leaf.

Health Care

As in most countries, the availability and quality of health care in Thailand varies between cities and rural areas and depends on a person's income. Several excellent hospitals provide a wide range of care. Some hospitals are involved with programs that work to improve nutrition in rural areas. They encourage pregnant women to take food supplements to ensure healthy babies. Women are also encouraged to breast-feed their babies to pass on antibodies, which fight diseases. They hope to reduce the infant mortality rate, which is about 18 deaths per 1,000 births.

The life expectancy for men is seventy-one years; it is seventy-five years for women. Since 2005 the life expectancy has increased about five years for men and two years for women. The leading causes of death in Thailand are heart and vascular diseases, cancers, and HIV/AIDS.

Heart and vascular diseases can lead to heart attacks and strokes. High blood pressure, high cholesterol, and obesity are the main causes of heart and vascular diseases.

Cancers can be caused by smoking, drinking too much alcohol, eating too many fatty foods, and not getting enough fiber. Foods high in fiber include fruits, vegetables, and grains.

HIV is usually spread by sharing needles when using illegal drugs or through risky sexual behavior. A person with HIV who does not eat a healthy diet will develop AIDS and die more quickly. At one time Thailand had one the world's highest rates of people both living with and dying from HIV/AIDS. Through government health and education programs, those rates have dropped to eighteenth (HIV) and seventeenth (AIDS) in the world.

Besides modern medicine and government health programs, Thailand has a long tradition of using herbal medicines. The flesh of many herbs, fruits, and vegetables are eaten to prevent or

Thailand's Nutritious Foods

Name	Taste	Health Benefits
Chilies	Mild to hot	Vitamins A, C; prevents and relieves colds, flu, congestion; aids blood circulation
Durian (King of Fruits)	Sweet, creamy with strong odor	Vitamins A, B, C, protein, iron, calcium
Galangal	Similar to ginger	Aids digestion
Kaffir lime skin and leaves	Bitter	Used to treat high blood pressure and to prevent cancer
Longan	Sweet, juicy	Vitamin C, calcium, iron, phosphorus; clears the complexion and boosts energy
Lychee	Sweet to tart, juicy	Vitamins B_1, B_2, C, iron, phosphorus, niacin; aids digestion, quenches thirst, alleviates anemia
Mangosteen (Queen of Fruits)	Sweet to tart segments	Vitamins B, C, calcium, niacin, phosphorus; aids wound healing, relieves swollen joints
Pomelo	Sweet to sour, juicy segments, similar to grapefruit	Fiber, vitamins A, B, C, calcium, phosphorus
Tamarind	Tart	Vitamins A, B, C, calcium; soothes coughs

relieve everything from cancer to the common cold. Skins, leaves, and seeds of other plants are ground into pastes. Their juices are important, too. Recently, mangosteen juice has been shown to relieve allergies, back pain, and joints swollen from arthritis.

Thailand has all the basic ingredients to be a healthy nation. First, the Thai people grow great amounts of a wide variety of healthy foods. Second, their government sponsors programs that are successfully reducing malnutrition and diseases. If the Thai can stop the obesity problem before it gets worse, they will reduce heart disease and cancer and will live longer, healthier, happier lives.

Glossary

alms food given freely as part of a religious belief

animism a belief that spirits exist in objects in nature such as water, rocks, and trees

cholesterol a waxy, fatlike substance that is both made by the body and found in food from animals

cuisine a style or way of cooking or presenting food

curry a soupy stew that receives much of its flavor from a paste made from chilies and herbs

fermented the strong, sour taste that occurs when fruits and vegetables age

klong a canal that is used for irrigation and transportation in Thailand

malnutrition a health problem caused by not eating enough healthy foods

merit a spiritual reward earned by doing good that will be applied to a Buddhist's existence in the next life

monarchy a form of government in which supreme power is held by one person

monsoon a strong wind that brings heavy rains or dry weather, depending on the direction from which it is blowing

mortar and pestle a small, thick bowl (mortar) and a short stick with a thick rounded end (pestle) that are used for grinding food into pastes; usually made of stone

obesity a physical condition in which a person is excessively fat or over-weight

talaat an open-air market that sells fresh fruits, vegetables, meats, fish, and seafood

wat a Buddhist temple, including both the place of worship and the area where its monks live

wok a metal cooking pan with a slightly rounded bottom and high sides

Find Out More

BOOKS

DeVoss, David. *A Portrait of Thailand.* New York: New Line Books Limited, 2006.

Locricchio, Matthew. *The Cooking of Thailand.* New York: Marshall Cavendish Benchmark, 2012.

Nuo, Johnny. *Duangkaew: Thai Village Girl.* Victoria, British Columbia: Trafford Publishing, 2005.

Rau, Dana Meachen. *Thailand.* New York: Marshall Cavendish Benchmark, 2007.

DVDS

Basic Fruit & Vegetable Carving. Produced by James Parker. Made on location in Thailand with Chef James Parker.

Learn to Cook Thai. Produced by SITCA on Koh Samui Island. Three DVDs present instructions for twelve authentic Thai recipes with ingredients available in the United States.

WEBSITES

Temple of Thai

www.templeofthai.com

This site includes a food store with pictures for ordering Thai ingredients. It also contains information about Thai cookware, lists of cookbooks with sample recipes, and instructions for fruit carving.

Thai Students Online

www.thaistudents.com

This site has more than five thousand pages covering everything from Thai culture, music, and language to tips on how to enjoy Songkran and of course food. The food pages have quizzes on identifying famous Thai dishes.

Thai Table

www.thaitable.com

This site includes not only recipes but also information about outdoor markets and street food.

Index

Page numbers in **boldface** are illustrations and charts.

About the Author

Patricia K. Kummer has a B.A. in history from the College of St. Catherine in St. Paul, Minnesota, and an M.A. in history from Marquette University in Milwaukee, Wisconsin. She has contributed chapters to several American and world history textbooks and has written more than sixty books about states, countries, inventions, and other topics. Books she has written for Marshall Cavendish include the revised editions of *Minnesota* and *Mississippi* in the Celebrate the States series and *The Great Barrier Reef* and *The Great Lakes* in the Nature's Wonders series.

Kummer always enjoys doing research for her books, and this book was no exception. She especially enjoyed sampling Thai foods at local restaurants and cooking Thai dishes at home. She hopes students will try the recipes in this book, which create a complete Thai meal. She would like to thank the staff at the Royal Thai Consulate-General in Chicago and the staff at the Thai Trade Center in Chicago for their help in providing recipes and numerous brochures about the food crops and dishes of Thailand.